The Business Response to Misconduct Allegations

The Business Response to Misconduct Allegations

Playbook

Third Edition

John D. Thompson, Esq.

AMSTERDAM · BOSTON · HEIDELBERG · LONDON
NEW YORK · OXFORD · PARIS · SAN DIEGO
ELSEVIER SAN FRANCISCO · SINGAPORE · SYDNEY · TOKYO

Security
Executive Council

Elsevier
The Boulevard, Langford Lane, Kidlington, Oxford, OX5 1GB, UK
225 Wyman Street, Waltham, MA 02451, USA

Originally published by the Security Executive Council, 2007

British Library Cataloguing in Publication Data
A catalogue record for this book is available from the British Library

Library of Congress Cataloging-in-Publication Data
A catalog record for this book is available from the Library of Congress

ISBN: 978-0-12-800841-6

For more publications in the Elsevier Risk Management and Security Collection,
visit our website at **store.elsevier.com/SecurityExecutiveCouncil**

This book has been manufactured using Print On Demand technology. Each copy is produced to order and is limited to black ink. The online version of this book will show color figures where appropriate.

Working together
to grow libraries in
developing countries

www.elsevier.com • www.bookaid.org

CONTENTS

Executive Summary.. ix

Section I Introduction 1
1.1 Who Is This Book for? 1
1.2 What Exactly Do We Mean by "Investigations?" 4

Section II Reasons to Investigate 7
2.1 Legal Requirement to Investigate...............................7
2.2 Legal "Knew or Should Have Known" Standard 8
2.3 Formal Versus Informal Complaint 9

Section III Preliminary Issues...11
3.1 Preliminary Interviews..11
3.2 Ensure the Safety of All Concerned...........................11

Section IV Creation of a Need-to-Know Group............................13

Section V Identification of Appropriate Investigators................15
5.1 Special Skills...15
5.2 Attorney–Client Privilege and Attorney Work Product............15
5.3 Conflicts of Interest 17
5.4 Objectivity and Pressures......................................17
5.5 Matching the Investigator to the Situation 18

Section VI Planning the Investigation 21
6.1 Minimize Witness Intimidation 22
6.2 Form Investigative Team and Divide Duties.....................22
6.3 Establish the Time Frame for the Investigation.................23
6.4 Confirmatory Memorandum 23
6.5 Obtain Relevant Documents 24
6.6 Special Investigative Techniques...............................26
6.7 Determine Who to Interview 26
6.8 Interview Location...27
6.9 Interview Order 27

6.10 Prepare Opening and Closing Comments 27
6.11 Prepare a Set of Written Questions.....................................28
6.12 Multiple Interviews...28
6.13 Written Statements 29
6.14 Taking Notes 29

Section VII General Interview Issues 31
7.1 Procedural Issues 31
7.2 Issues Unique to Public Entities 36
7.3 Specific Issues 38
7.4 Style Issues..46
7.5 Issues Unique to the Subject Matter.....................................47

Section VIII Taking Notes 51
8.1 Designate a Primary Note Taker..51
8.2 What to Include in Notes 51
8.3 Need for Completeness...51
8.4 Exclude Interpretation, Subjective Comments or Conclusions ...52
8.5 Note Demeanor 52
8.6 Write for the Jury 52

Section IX Taking Written Statements 55
9.1 Obtaining Voluntary Statements 55
9.2 Requiring Employee Statements...55
9.3 Identify Topics but Not Content 56
9.4 Elements of the Statement 56

Section X Reporting Findings 59
10.1 Reporting Preliminary Conclusions 59
10.2 Inclusion of Attorney..60
10.3 Reporting Conclusions, Recommendations 60
10.4 After Consensus Is Reached, Create a Summary Report..........61
10.5 Communication Beyond the Need-to-Know Group 61
10.6 Attorney File Review...61

Section XI Investigations in Union Environments....................63
11.1 Handling the Press..63
11.2 Conclusion 64

Appendix A: Checklists 65

Appendix B: Sample Confirmation Memorandum 69

Appendix C: Investigation Matrix 71

About the Author 77

About Elsevier's Security Executive Council
Risk Management Portfolio 79

Industry Applicability Validation 81

The Business Response to Misconduct Allegations playbook, third edition, has been created for business professionals who are the first to be contacted during a suspected employee-related claim and who may not have had investigative training. It is a step-by-step guide of what to do—and, perhaps more importantly, what *not* to do—in laying the groundwork of an investigation. Sections of this playbook discuss considerations when deciding whether to investigate, preliminary issues, naming investigators, investigative planning, interview techniques and issues, the importance of taking notes and written statements, and much more.

Also included are a series of checklists and templates to aid the investigative team before, during, and after the investigation concludes. This playbook is an essential risk management resource for audit professionals, business conduct and compliance professionals, facility or building managers, human resources professionals, information technology security professionals, and any others who may be the first to receive reports of wrongdoing, regulatory violations, or allegations about workforce behavior.

WHAT IS A PLAYBOOK?

A playbook is an excellent tool for the security or business leader to develop, implement, or enhance a specific aspect of a security or risk management program; in this case, compliance response. Playbooks provide a short, detailed treatment of a specific security program or service and explain why it is important to the business. They present the essentials—a framework of best practices the security professional can use to set up, manage, and explain the program to stakeholders. Playbooks also provide templates, forms, and checklists for immediate adaptation. A playbook may be used by security professionals who need an introduction and plan for action on a new job responsibility, or by educators and business people who need an overview of a security area.

Introduction

1.1 WHO IS THIS BOOK FOR? 1

1.1.1 Audit Professionals 2

1.1.2 Compliance Professionals 2

1.1.3 Facilities and Building Managers 3

1.1.4 Human Resources Professionals 3

1.1.5 Information Technology Security Professionals 4

1.2 WHAT EXACTLY DO WE MEAN BY "INVESTIGATIONS?" 4

1.1 WHO IS THIS BOOK FOR?

This playbook is written for business people who do not have training or have little experience in the initial handling of reported incidents relating to employee conduct. It is important to know the initial actions to take, what steps to follow, and what *not* to do when an employee comes to you with a complaint that requires further investigation. Even if a company has security professionals dedicated to this endeavor, it's possible that they cannot conduct every investigation that the organization requires and therefore, business conduct and compliance professionals are called upon to assist (for example). The sections in this playbook provide a process to ensure a successful investigation.

The need for conducting or assisting in a related investigation might arise from an anonymous hotline call, a complaint to the security professional or other colleague in the company. The correctness of the actions taken is dependent in large measure upon the quality of the case that the investigator conducts or leads. Well-conducted investigations are essential to protecting the organization legally, protecting the rights of employees, and observing the organization's human resources policies and principles.

The following sections outline what roles certain business professionals may play in investigations.

1.1.1 Audit Professionals

Audit professionals are responsible for overseeing the internal risk management controls and governance processes that are in place. These professionals work to preserve the organization's values. The benefit of assisting with or completing a proficient investigation is to uphold these values and possibly prevent brand reputation damage.

Typically audit professionals are asked to assist with the following employee-related investigations:

- Regulatory violations
- Compliance with law or organization policy
- Theft/fraud
- Trade secrets
- Whistleblower
- Business ethics or business conduct
- Insider trading or securities violations
- Contract violations
- Mergers and acquisitions, including due diligence

1.1.2 Compliance Professionals

Compliance professionals are responsible for the corporation's business strategies, policies, standards, and practices related to the organization's compliance and ethics function. One area on their watch is potential workplace harassment or other violations of their organization's human resources policies.

Typically business conduct and compliance professionals are asked to assist with the following employee-related investigations:

- Harassment
- Discrimination
- Employee theft
- Workplace violence
- Trade secrets
- Wage and hour violations
- Whistleblowing
- Employee discipline
- Wrongful termination
- Employee vs. independent contractor status
- Business ethics or business conduct

- Insider trading or securities violations
- Mergers and acquisitions, including due diligence
- Compliance with law or organization policy

1.1.3 Facilities and Building Managers

Facilities and building managers are responsible for building and equipment maintenance, emergency procedures and general employee safety. One area on their watch may be employee conduct that risks business property or other employees.

Typically a facilities or building manager will be the first person to whom an incident will be reported. This includes incidents such as:

- Workplace violence
- Harassment
- Intimidation
- Threats (including bomb threats)
- Assaults
- Robbery and burglaries
- Construction fraud
- Safety violations
- Suspicious items
- Warrants
- Police notifications
- Falsification of time cards/billing hours

1.1.4 Human Resources Professionals

Busy human resources (HR) professionals hear many employee concerns over the course of a day. Many times human emotions run deep. Their guidance and processes related to employee well-being are an important part of keeping the organization humming. HR professionals may be involved with the initial handling of reported incidents relating to employee conduct.

Typically HR professionals will be asked to assist with the following employee-related investigations:

- Harassment
- Discrimination
- Employee theft
- Workplace violence

- Trade secrets
- Wage and hour violations
- Whistleblower
- Employee discipline
- Wrongful termination
- Employee vs. independent contractor status
- Business ethics or business conduct
- Insider trading or securities violations
- Mergers and acquisitions, including due diligence
- Compliance with law or organization policy

1.1.5 Information Technology Security Professionals

Information technology (IT) security professionals involved in investigations may include line managers and supervisors, in the technical or operational side of the organization. Investigators often will become involved in investigations of potential workplace harassment or other violations of their organization's human resources policies.

Typically IT security professionals will be asked to assist with employee-related investigations. Examples include:

- Inappropriate use of systems, applications or the internet
- Prohibited material on company equipment
- Information, software or hardware theft
- Loss of or disclosure of confidential or proprietary information
- Trade secrets or pending patent disclosures
- Vendor billing frauds
- Whistleblower complaints
- Employee threats, harassment, or intimidation using email
- Responding to court orders for email, documents, or instant message logs
- Insider criminal activity
- Business ethics or business conduct violations
- Insider trading or securities violations
- Mergers and acquisitions information leakage
- Compliance with laws or organization policy

1.2 WHAT EXACTLY DO WE MEAN BY "INVESTIGATIONS?"

By investigations, we mean fact finding, often for others who will make decisions based upon the results of your fact finding efforts.

Obviously, many issues do not require investigations and many other issues require the consultation or involvement of persons other than an investigator. Some of the advice in this guide reflects lessons learned when the spotlight of litigation has been placed upon an investigator's practices. It is hoped that these materials will yield better investigations, better decisions and, yes, fewer and more defensible lawsuits.

The key to a successful investigation is planning. With that in mind, included at the end of this guide are several checklists that serve as a reminder of the various considerations outlined as the investigator plans and carries out an investigation. (Note: See Appendix C: Investigation Matrix, a consolidation of checklists and other information in a fully usable spreadsheet to document the steps of each investigation.)

It should be noted that this guide does not intend to convey legal advice. As well, the appropriate scope and manner of any investigation will depend upon the particular circumstances of the situation as well as the location of the investigation. It is intended to provide general guidelines and considerations for investigators confronted with the often difficult task of conducting an employee-related investigation.

Reasons to Investigate

2.1 LEGAL REQUIREMENT TO INVESTIGATE **7**

2.2 LEGAL "KNEW OR SHOULD HAVE KNOWN" STANDARD **8**

2.3 FORMAL VERSUS INFORMAL COMPLAINT **9**

When an employee or a third party claims that one of the organization's policies has been violated, the first decision the organization must make is whether the issue deserves further investigation.

2.1 LEGAL REQUIREMENT TO INVESTIGATE

The following issues frequently come to the attention of the organization and normally must be investigated by the organization either because the law imposes a duty to investigate, or the law holds the organization liable for any consequences of its failure to investigate and correct a problem:

- Harassment
- Discrimination
- Potentially violent employees
- Criminal violations
- Organizational policy violations

All claims or evidence of criminal violations must be investigated by the organization. The investigator should contact legal counsel immediately when they learn of a possible criminal violation.

There are many legal and nonlegal reasons to investigate alleged violations of an organization's human resources policies:

- Protecting the rights of employees
- Employee relations benefits
- Obligation to uphold the organization's human resources principles
- Determining the facts
- Determining the appropriate response to the situation

- Determining the potential criminal and civil liability of the organization and any managers or supervisors involved
- Determining whether the organization has any legal defenses to any potential claims
- Reducing civil liability by demonstrating a good-faith response to the issue
- Possible public relations benefits

There also are several reasons *not* to investigate certain alleged violations of human resources policies:

- For whatever reason, corrective action by management is not possible or within the organization's control.
- The misconduct or issue involved is not sufficiently serious.
- The matter can be resolved satisfactorily by another means, such as counseling.
- The allegation lacks credibility on its face.

Frequently, in the course of investigating one issue, investigators will uncover additional allegations of a violation of law or organizational policy. Even though these are outside the scope of the original investigation, the organization might have a legal or policy obligation to investigate the additional allegations. Whoever is conducting the investigation should flag these so that the organization can make a judgment as to whether to investigate the additional allegations. Significant liability for the organization can occur if there is no follow up. Often, these other allegations can be investigated at a later time, but in general should not be ignored.

2.2 LEGAL "KNEW OR SHOULD HAVE KNOWN" STANDARD

The employment laws relating to harassment and discrimination, as well as other laws, impose liability upon employers when they "knew or should have known" about a problem and did not take appropriate action to solve the problem. Until the investigator is certain that he or she possesses all of the information available to evaluate the issue appropriately, the investigation should continue. Many human resources problems, not to mention lawsuits, develop because a complaint is made and no investigation occurs and the complaint is not dealt with in an appropriate manner.

For example, if the investigator does not really know how badly an employee was harassed, the organization does not know whether only a verbal reprimand to the harasser is appropriate or something stronger is required. The legal and human resources risk is not just the failure to investigate, but the failure to prevent further harassment.

2.3 FORMAL VERSUS INFORMAL COMPLAINT

Frequently, the complaining individual indicates that he or she does not want to make a formal complaint, is not making a formal complaint, does not want the investigator to take any action, or wants the investigator to keep the complaint confidential. Even in these cases, the investigator should investigate the complaint and take appropriate action. The investigator and the organization are "on notice." The investigator should tell complaining individuals in these circumstances that the organization is legally obligated to investigate their complaint and to do so promptly and that it might be legally liable if prompt and appropriate action is not taken to investigate the information provided.

Consider the following scenario: Sally comes to her boss and complains that her coworker Jim is making passes at her on business trips and once even asked her to join him in his hotel room. Sally then tells her boss that she can handle Jim, and that she brought it up only as a "heads up" to her boss in case it gets worse. The boss, satisfied that Sally can handle herself, does nothing about this complaint. On the next business trip, Jim sexually assaults Sally. Do you think the organization has legal liability?

Preliminary Issues

3.1 PRELIMINARY INTERVIEWS 11

3.2 ENSURE THE SAFETY OF ALL CONCERNED 11

3.1 PRELIMINARY INTERVIEWS

An investigator should ask some follow-up questions of any individual who makes a formal complaint, informal complaint, memo, email, off-hand remark, or other comment that suggests a possible violation of the law or organization policy. If an individual's statement reasonably implies a problem, the investigator should investigate further by asking enough questions to determine whether a problem really exists or whether the issue requires further investigation.

3.2 ENSURE THE SAFETY OF ALL CONCERNED

One essential part of any preliminary interview is to determine whether any immediate safety issues exist. Sometimes, the information learned from the complainant suggests that there might be a danger to someone's safety. If the situation is potentially dangerous, the first and immediate objective should be to take whatever steps are necessary to reduce or eliminate the danger. Except in extreme emergencies, this should be accomplished by consultation with legal counsel. There might be times, for example, when it is appropriate to take measures to ensure the safety of the complainant before the investigator has investigated the validity of the complainant's allegations.

Creation of a Need-to-Know Group

As an initial part of any investigation, it is critical to identify the group of people who have a business need to know about the issue and who should participate in developing an appropriate response to the situation. The organization should determine who needs to know about the complaint, what they need to know about it, and when they need to know. This group is called the need-to-know group.

The purpose of identifying this need-to-know group is to protect the confidentiality of the situation, the identity of the people involved, the investigation process and the results of the investigation. (Of course, the need-to-know group also usually is the set of decision-makers who will evaluate the situation, the results of any investigation, and the appropriateness of any action to take.) Communications about an individual (e.g., an alleged wrongdoer) beyond this need-to-know group increases the risk of defamation claims if the communications turn out to be false.[1] Additionally, liability risks may also exist if truthful information about individuals involved in the investigation is unnecessarily shared outside of the need-to-know group.

In identifying the need-to-know group, the organization should exclude any individuals who are involved directly in the issue, such as an alleged victim, wrongdoer, or witness. When decision-makers have a stake in the resolution of the issue, the complaining or affected individual (or a judge or jury) might view them as biased or not

---

[1] To establish the tort of defamation, a plaintiff must prove that a false and defamatory statement of fact was published to a third party and no legal privilege exists. Employers typically have a legal privilege for any comment made as part of an investigation if they can establish that they had reasonable cause to make the comment, they made the comment in good faith, and the comment was made on a proper occasion. If the comment is made to someone not in the need-to-know group, it is much more difficult to prove that the comment was made on a proper occasion. As with most common law claims, the law of defamation varies from state to state and the investigator should seek legal counsel for the applicable law.

completely objective.[2] It also is important for the need-to-know group to evaluate witnesses candidly, which is more difficult when the witnesses are evaluating themselves. This notion of excluding those with a conflict of interest recurs when the organization is determining who should conduct the investigation, to which we now turn. (*Note*: Appendix C: Investigation Matrix is a spreadsheet compiling much of the specific information and checklists in upcoming sections.)

[2]Thus, it is critical that anyone who might be viewed as biased be removed from the need-to-know group at the earliest possible moment. For example, what if a potential target of the investigation plays a role in selecting the investigator, and later is removed from any further involvement in the investigation? That initial involvement will be argued to taint the entire investigation. At that point, it would be appropriate to select another investigator just to take away the claim of a tainted investigation, even if the original investigator was perfectly appropriate.

Identification of Appropriate Investigators

5.1 SPECIAL SKILLS 15
5.2 ATTORNEY–CLIENT PRIVILEGE AND ATTORNEY WORK
    PRODUCT.. 15
5.3 CONFLICTS OF INTEREST 17
5.4 OBJECTIVITY AND PRESSURES 17
5.5 MATCHING THE INVESTIGATOR TO THE SITUATION 18

Before any investigation begins, the organization must identify the appropriate human resources individual(s)—or others—to conduct the investigation. To identify the appropriate investigator or investigative team, the organization should consider the following issues.

5.1 SPECIAL SKILLS

Investigations into certain activities require special investigative skills such as those of legal counsel, public law enforcement personnel, computer security experts, or threat assessment experts:

- Complex or novel criminal activity (e.g., fraud, drug sales, business information losses, computer hacking, and theft of trade secrets)
- Potentially violent employees

If the investigating professional obtains any information concerning possible criminal activity, he or she should provide that information immediately to legal counsel.

5.2 ATTORNEY–CLIENT PRIVILEGE AND ATTORNEY WORK PRODUCT

Every once in a while, the organization might decide that an investigation involves significant legal risk to the corporation. In this case, legal counsel should exercise tight control over the investigation in order to maximize the organization's claim that the information developed by the investigation is protected from disclosure to third parties by virtue of the attorney–client privilege and attorney work product doctrine.[1]

The attorney–client privilege involves communications between attorney and client if the client is seeking legal advice from the attorney and the attorney is providing legal advice to the client. If the communication is privileged, it need not be revealed to any third party. It should be noted, however, that the privilege does not involve the underlying facts obtained in the investigation. For example, suppose that during the course of a discussion between attorney and client, the client states that 17% of its widgets manufacturing violates the law. That discussion is privileged and need not be revealed to a third party. But the fact that 17% of the widgets have certain characteristics that are in violation of the law will have to be revealed to third parties. The privilege, however, makes it hard for third parties to obtain discovery or investigate the issues.

The attorney work product acts to prevent disclosure of certain information created as a result of an attorney's investigation into the facts of a situation. If an attorney conducts an interview, for example, his or her notes of that interview are arguably protected from disclosure to third parties. An attorney need not reveal his "mental impressions," which frequently are memorialized in notes during interviews. Again, the underlying comments by the interviewee are still discoverable and the attorney might have to produce excerpts from his notes that merely quote the interviewee. This doctrine makes it harder for third parties to obtain discovery or investigate the issues. If attorneys conduct the investigation, their notes have a much greater chance of remaining out of the hands of a plaintiff or other person who wants to learn about the facts.

There are also investigations that will call for the special investigative skills of an attorney, for example, if they are subject-matter experts on particular topics. If the investigation involves complex laws or

---

[1] Again, it is critical that the organization makes this decision at the outset. All too often, the horse leaves the barn before the organization's attorney has an opportunity to take control over the investigation, or at least control the flow of communications. If in doubt, the investigator should give the organization's legal counsel the opportunity to review the situation. The way to do this is either to pick up the telephone and talk to the attorney, or begin a written communication with the following sentence: "I am writing to you to request legal advice regarding a situation that just came to my attention."

regulations, an attorney might be the appropriate questioner to make sure that, legally, the correct questions are asked.

Note: *Even if the organization's legal counsel does not conduct the investigation, it is frequently the case that the organization will want the attorney to have overall control of the investigation, and request other investigators to conduct the investigation on the attorney's behalf so that the attorney can provide legal advice to the company. Under the law, this approach maximizes the chances that the investigation would have to be disclosed to third parties.*

5.3 CONFLICTS OF INTEREST

It is difficult to discuss the topic of conflicts of interest in a few paragraphs. In general, every investigation should consider this issue at the outset. Are there actual conflicts of interest between interested parties in the investigation? How does your organization define a conflict of interest?

There are several types of conflicts of interest. There are *actual* conflicts of interest. For example, if a complaint alleges that a particular individual has committed misconduct of some type, obviously the accused wrongdoer should not be the investigator. The organization might want to define an actual conflict of interest broadly. That is, it might want to prevent any individual remotely involved in the allegation from participating in the investigation.

There also are *potential* conflicts of interest. Organizations should closely examine situations for potential conflicts of interest, because many potential conflicts of interest have a nasty habit of becoming actual conflicts, which normally has the undesirable side effect of requiring you to start your investigation or decision-making all over again.

There is no real road map to identifying potential conflicts of interest. Organizations need to use common sense about what direction or directions an investigation might go. If there is anyone who has a stake in the outcome that also has the role of an objective decision-maker or investigator, that person should be excluded from the process out of an abundance of caution.

5.4 OBJECTIVITY AND PRESSURES

The individual about to conduct the investigation must ask himself or herself whether he or she is and can be objective about the subject matter of the investigation. If the investigator has any bias or for whatever reason has some predisposition as to the outcome of the investigation, he or she should not be the investigator. It is, of course, perfectly permissible for the investigator to have a hypothesis or theory that he or she will test during the investigation. But the investigator must always be able to reject or alter that hypothesis when he or she obtains information inconsistent with that hypothesis.

Similarly, the individual conducting the investigation must be as free as possible from pressures that would intimidate or incentivize the investigator to slant his or her views or conduct. These pressures can come from many directions. It could come from the accused wrongdoer. It could come from the government. It could come from some strongly-held belief of the investigator, for example, a religious belief. It could come from upper management. The organization's leaders must be confident that the individuals conducting their investigations will conduct themselves objectively and withstand the pressures common to many investigations.

5.5 MATCHING THE INVESTIGATOR TO THE SITUATION

The investigator should be matched to the situation. For example, if any important party involved in the investigation believes that the investigator is biased, the reduced level of trust might reduce the amount of information the investigator obtains. Even worse, if someone does not like the outcome of the investigation and seeks to challenge the fairness or legality of the process, it is likely they will use this perceived bias as part of their legal argument. It is best to address all claims of bias in a matter designed to eliminate bias as well as the potential legal arguments of litigants attacking the organization.

The organization should seek to utilize investigators who can derive the maximum amount of information from interviewees. This is likely a skill the human resources professional has. Although, there are other factors to consider, such as gender. For example, many times victims of sexual harassment are more forthcoming to an interviewer of their own sex—because victims sometimes generalize feelings about the harasser to the harasser's entire gender. Frequently, victims are more willing to "open up" to interviewers of the same gender.

The following should serve as a checklist whenever the organization is determining who should conduct an investigation.

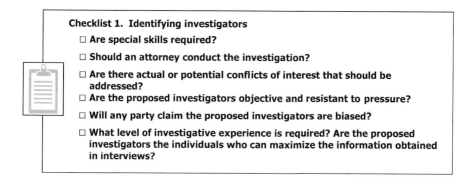

Checklist 1. Identifying investigators
- ☐ **Are special skills required?**
- ☐ **Should an attorney conduct the investigation?**
- ☐ **Are there actual or potential conflicts of interest that should be addressed?**
- ☐ **Are the proposed investigators objective and resistant to pressure?**
- ☐ **Will any party claim the proposed investigators are biased?**
- ☐ **What level of investigative experience is required? Are the proposed investigators the individuals who can maximize the information obtained in interviews?**

It is also worthwhile mentioning that some companies decide to contract out investigations and retain an outside professional investigator. In this circumstance, it is critical to conduct a proper due diligence review of the contract investigator's credentials and background. All contract investigators should sign a nondisclosure agreement.

Planning the Investigation

6.1 MINIMIZE WITNESS INTIMIDATION.. 22

6.2 FORM INVESTIGATIVE TEAM AND DIVIDE DUTIES.................... 22

6.3 ESTABLISH THE TIME FRAME FOR THE INVESTIGATION......... 23

6.4 CONFIRMATORY MEMORANDUM.. 23

6.5 OBTAIN RELEVANT DOCUMENTS.. 24

6.6 SPECIAL INVESTIGATIVE TECHNIQUES.................................... 26

6.7 DETERMINE WHO TO INTERVIEW.. 26

6.8 INTERVIEW LOCATION... 27

6.9 INTERVIEW ORDER... 27

6.10 PREPARE OPENING AND CLOSING COMMENTS...................... 27

6.11 PREPARE A SET OF WRITTEN QUESTIONS................................ 28

6.12 MULTIPLE INTERVIEWS... 28

6.13 WRITTEN STATEMENTS.. 29

6.14 TAKING NOTES... 29

The objective of an investigation is to get the facts so that a resolution of the complaint and situation can be achieved. At the same time, it is possible that someday a jury or attorneys outside the organization might scrutinize every aspect of any investigation conducted. For example, the organization might have to turn over every note the investigator has taken during the investigation to outside attorneys, and the investigator might have to recount every conversation he or she had involving the investigation. Moreover, someone's job or well-being might depend upon the quality of the investigation. Thus, an investigation is not something that should be done haphazardly or without a clear plan in mind.

> *Many investigators have declared their embarrassment to me when I have reviewed their investigation file two years after the investigation in preparation for a deposition or trial testimony. The investigator's memory naturally is poor about the investigation because it is years later and numerous investigations have come and gone in the interim period. To make matters worse, the investigator's notes are often cryptic, undated, and virtually useless. What seemed like a perfectly reasonable investigation plan at the time is impossible to decipher later. Because every part of an investigation might later be subject to scrutiny, every part of the investigation should be documented, including the up-front planning process.*

The following considerations should help the investigator plan an investigation. This, in turn, should lead to more accurate and complete information obtained and greater legal protection for the organization.

6.1 MINIMIZE WITNESS INTIMIDATION

As the investigator begins thinking about how to conduct the investigation, he or she must confront the possibility that certain witnesses to the investigation might feel intimidated by the alleged wrongdoer, even by the simple fact that the alleged wrongdoer is in the workplace. Even worse, the alleged wrongdoer (and even the complainant) might intimidate, harass, or retaliate against witnesses in an attempt to influence the outcome of the investigation.

It might be necessary to remove the alleged wrongdoer, the complainant or both individuals in order to maximize the information obtainable from other witnesses. On the other hand, removing an employee from the workplace during an investigation is a serious human resources matter. If the investigator believes that removing an employee from the workplace is necessary to remove possible intimidation, he or she should consider consulting with the need-to-know group to obtain a consensus on such an action.[1]

6.2 FORM INVESTIGATIVE TEAM AND DIVIDE DUTIES

Interviews often will constitute a major part of the investigation, and it could be a serious mistake to conduct significant interviews one-on-one. If the investigation is legally challenged, the plaintiff inevitably

---

[1]The investigator should arrange the investigation environment so as to minimize even the appearance of intimidation whenever possible.

will contest the accuracy of the interviewer's recollection of the interview. If the organization has two witnesses to interview who have similar recollections, it will be more difficult for the plaintiff to attack the credibility of the investigation.

Moreover, it is extremely difficult to ask intelligent questions, listen closely to the answers, formulate follow-up questions, and take accurate notes all at the same time. A solution would be to have two interviewers, where one interviewer is responsible for the questioning and the other interviewer is responsible for note taking. The note taker also can ask follow-up questions that the primary questioner might miss. This division of responsibility should remain consistent throughout the interview process.

Two interviewers will give you two different perspectives on the situation. Many difficult investigations require tough credibility judgments and it would be valuable to know, for example, that two interviewers have different perspectives on the credibility of a key witness.

6.3 ESTABLISH THE TIME FRAME FOR THE INVESTIGATION

Many times, the organization can avoid liability for wrongs committed by its employees, even supervisory employees, if management takes quick and appropriate action to remedy the situation. Thus, it is always desirable to conduct the investigation promptly after becoming aware of the issue.[2] Impress upon others the need to investigate and resolve the issue quickly and obtain the cooperation necessary to have interviewees available. Of course, if the investigation becomes more complicated than anticipated or unanticipated delays occur, extend the deadline if necessary to do a complete investigation.

6.4 CONFIRMATORY MEMORANDUM

The investigator must determine whether to provide the complainant with a confirmatory memorandum. This is frequently desirable when the complainant raises a verbal complaint. The memorandum serves a

[2]The definition of promptly, of course, depends upon the situation. A victim of harassment might claim that an investigation that took 3 days is too long. On the other hand, if the investigation does not directly involve the complainant's well-being, a much longer time frame might be justifiable.

variety of purposes. Most importantly, it provides the complainant with a clear understanding of the expectations that the organization has for him or her during the investigation. A letter to the complainant should include the following items:

1. A statement confirming the issues that the complainant has raised.
2. A list of all facts provided by the complainant.
3. A request that the complainant add, delete, or correct the facts summarized and a confidential means to provide this information.
4. A statement identifying the investigator(s) and confirming that the complainant has agreed the investigator(s) will be fair and objective. If the identity of the investigator(s) was not previously known to the complainant, the letter should include a statement that the complainant finds the investigator(s) to be fair and objective unless the complainant indicates otherwise.
5. The anticipated time frame of the investigation and the method and timing of feedback from the investigator(s).
6. A statement that the complainant's cooperation and participation in the investigation is required.
7. A statement that the complainant should not discuss this matter further (other than with the investigator(s)) while the investigation is being conducted, particularly within the organization.
8. A statement of the consequences of the complainant's failure to follow these instructions. The consequences will depend upon whether the complainant is an employee or third party.

Note: An example of such a confirmation letter is contained in Appendix B.

6.5 OBTAIN RELEVANT DOCUMENTS

In many investigations, there is a paper trail that provides important information for the investigation. The documents the investigator reviews will answer many questions, raise many other important questions that the investigator will want to ask, identify individuals that the investigator will want to interview, and so on. The following is a checklist of internal documents that the investigator should consider obtaining:

Checklist 2 . Obtaining documents

☐ **Personnel files**

☐ **Telephone records**

☐ **Expense account records**

☐ **Personnel information on computer**

☐ **Appointment calendars**

☐ **Time cards**

☐ **Building entrance/exit records**

☐ **Computer/word processing disks (and hard drive memory)**

☐ **Electronic mail records**

☐ **Voice mail records**

This is just a sample. The investigator must create a checklist of types of documents potentially relevant to the investigation as part of the planning process—all interviewees should be asked for all possible relevant documents.

Before obtaining any information or documents that an employee might claim are private, contact legal counsel. For example, employees might claim that the organization has no right to obtain information found in their computer, computer disks, voice mail, electronic mail, briefcase, desk, file cabinets, and so on.

Information and other documents might exist outside of the organization that are relevant to the investigation. Obtaining such information could pose significant legal risk, and the investigator should not do so without consulting legal counsel. The following are examples of external information that might be available and relevant to your investigation:

- Commercially available computerized databases
- Public record checks
- Customer or vendor information

6.6 SPECIAL INVESTIGATIVE TECHNIQUES

With respect to many investigations, gathering relevant documents and interviewing relevant individuals will be the extent of the investigation conducted. Sequentially, the investigator should review the relevant documents obtained from the organization and then plan for the interview process. Therefore, the remainder of this section discusses planning for the interview process. However, there are certain times when special investigative techniques beyond mere interviews are appropriate. *These are almost always investigative techniques that have a high legal risk and never should be discussed or implemented without legal counsel.* In fact, many of these techniques should require high-level approval before they may be utilized, including the following:

• Internal audit
• Physical investigation (e.g., fingerprint, handwriting, voice analysis)
• Physical surveillance
• Polygraphs
• Searches of organization or private property
• Electronic monitoring or surveillance

6.7 DETERMINE WHO TO INTERVIEW

This list will grow and change during the course of the investigation, but at the outset the investigator should create an initial list of whom to interview. Be over inclusive rather than under inclusive when making this list. If there is any doubt about whether an individual might have relevant information for the investigation, include that individual on the list. To do otherwise will open the investigation to challenge as incomplete or biased. Often, the investigator will want to interview an entire department or work unit.

For example, if an employee alleges workplace harassment, the investigator will want to know if anyone else in the workplace has witnessed anything relevant to proving or disproving this allegation or has experienced similar harassment. A proven and successful investigative strategy for interviewing numerous employees in a large group is to select a cross section from the organization. This strategy also allows for specific individuals to be interviewed while appearing to be a part of the general cross section.

6.8 INTERVIEW LOCATION

The location of interviews can be the key to their success or failure. The need for confidentiality might necessitate conducting interviews away from the organization. Employees might be less candid with the interviewer if they believe that other employees are aware that they are being interviewed. Similarly, if employees can provide information anonymously there is less opportunity for others to pressure them into changing their story and less opportunity for retaliation against them. Ask witnesses if they are comfortable with the location of the interview and move the interview to another location if a witness indicates that he or she is not comfortable.

If the investigator is going to interview individuals away from the organization's facilities, never interview one-on-one in a hotel room or a private home. All one-on-one interviews away from the organization's facility (which should occur only rarely) should take place in a public place like a business office. Otherwise, the investigator might needlessly subject himself or herself to false claims of inappropriate conduct that would be difficult to disprove.

6.9 INTERVIEW ORDER

Correctly ordering the sequence of interviews can improve the efficiency and quality of any investigation. Do not order interviews based simply upon the availability of the interviewees. In the context of a harassment claim, for example, it is often best to interview the alleged victim first, the alleged harasser next and then potential witnesses. In other contexts, it is often best to interview first a management-level employee who can provide an overview of the situation, a history of the parties involved, a sense as to what might have happened, and so on. The order of interviews will depend upon the unique facts of each investigation.

6.10 PREPARE OPENING AND CLOSING COMMENTS

For each interview, the investigator will want to have a set of opening comments and instructions, further discussed below. Similarly, the investigator will want to have a set of closing comments and instructions.

> *This is the part of the interview that is "canned" and not really dependent upon what any particular individual says. Therefore, there is no excuse for being unprepared or "missing" a particular point. For example, I once had a witness claim that she was being retaliated against after an interview. When asked why she did not immediately report the retaliation, her answer was that she didn't know that she should and didn't know to whom to report it. If true, the investigator was at fault for not providing this information to her as part of the "canned" opening and closing comments.*

6.11 PREPARE A SET OF WRITTEN QUESTIONS

This has several advantages. First, it will require the investigator to think carefully in advance about what information is needed, how best to elicit information from each individual, and how to protect the confidentiality of parties. Second, it will permit the investigator to organize the interview and develop a logical sequence for questions. Third, it enables the investigator to ask precisely the same questions to multiple individuals and ensures that the investigator will not forget asking certain questions.

The investigator must be careful, however, not to be so tied to an outline that he or she fails to ask necessary follow-up questions, or explore something identified by a witness that was not in the outline.[3]

6.12 MULTIPLE INTERVIEWS

It is a rare investigation that resolves all questions after interviewing witnesses only once. First, the investigator will frequently learn new information later in the investigation process that he or she will need to discuss with previously interviewed individuals. Second, multiple interviews are an excellent way to assess credibility. Challenging an individual with contrary information, asking the same question in a slightly different way or asking about information learned since your first interview of the individual can give a better assessment of the credibility of that individual.

---

[3]In reviewing investigative interviews after the fact, the most common failing is not to follow up on answers that the interviewee gives. Often, the interviewee's answers are unresponsive, partial, or vague. The skilled interviewer recognizes the unresponsiveness and asks follow-up questions until the question is answered completely.

Occasionally, the investigator might want to involve different interviewers to conduct a second round of interviews. This is appropriate if the first set of interviewers might have missed or been unable to obtain some critical information, or if it provides a valuable new perspective on the situation or if they possess different investigative skills, and so on. This approach also has drawbacks, such as creating more potential organization witnesses in any subsequent litigation. Do not adopt this approach without consulting with legal counsel.

There may be situations that call for simultaneous interviews of individuals, ensuring that the individuals do not have the opportunity to contact each other prior to the interview. This situation can be addressed either by having the first interviewee remain in a room with a witness until the second interview starts or by having simultaneous interviews by qualified investigators.

6.13 WRITTEN STATEMENTS

Written statements minimize the opportunity for interviewees to dispute the investigator's recollection of the interview or change their story. Statements also are a highly persuasive form of evidence. Many plaintiff lawyers have backed off when shown statements of several individuals refuting their client's story. Consult with legal counsel about this decision. If the investigator decides to take statements, see the section below on how to do this.

6.14 TAKING NOTES

If the investigation is later challenged legally, the organization will be asked to defend the fairness and quality of the investigative process. The plaintiff will argue that the organization came to the wrong result because the investigator did a poor investigation. The investigation will be more legally defensible if the organization can demonstrate that the investigator *planned* the investigation process, that the investigator considered each of the issues discussed in this section, and that the investigator had rational reasons for following or not following the suggestions contained in this section. As always, contemporaneous notes about how the investigation was planned will be more accurate and credible to a jury or judge than oral testimony at a later point.

Checklist 3. Planning the investigation

☐ Minimize witness intimidation

☐ Form investigative team and divide duties

☐ Establish time frame for investigation

☐ Prepare confirmatory memorandum

☐ Obtain relevant documents

☐ Consider special investigative techniques

☐ Identify interviewees

☐ Identify interview location

☐ Arrange interview order

☐ Prepare opening and closing comments

☐ Prepare set of written questions

☐ Plan for multiple interviews

☐ Decide whether to obtain written statements

☐ Take detailed notes of planning process

General Interview Issues

7.1 PROCEDURAL ISSUES **31**

7.2 ISSUES UNIQUE TO PUBLIC ENTITIES **36**

7.3 SPECIFIC ISSUES **38**

7.4 STYLE ISSUES **46**

7.5 ISSUES UNIQUE TO THE SUBJECT MATTER **47**

Now that the investigator has planned the interview process, the investigation is ready to begin. But there are a number of procedural, technical, and style issues that will make the interviews better and reduce the legal risks associated with the investigative process.

7.1 PROCEDURAL ISSUES

There are a number of procedural items to cover with each and every interviewee at the outset of any interview. Failure to cover these issues can lead to legal liability, low employee morale, and a failed investigation.

7.1.1 General Description of Situation

The investigator should generally describe to each interviewee the issue(s) involved in the investigation, an explanation of the investigator's position in the organization if the interviewee is unfamiliar with that and the fact that the interviewee is a potential witness to the issue(s) under investigation.

7.1.2 Purpose of Investigation

The investigator should make it clear to interviewees that the purpose of the investigation is to determine the facts and that the investigator is a fact finder, not a decision maker.

7.1.3 No Conclusions Reached

The investigator must make clear at the outset (and throughout the investigation) that he or she has not reached any conclusions as to what occurred, who is at fault, and so on. One of the most powerful indictments of an investigator is that the investigator made up his or her mind before gathering all of the facts, resulting in a biased assessment and a lack of both due process and fundamental fairness in the process.

The most common point at which the investigator makes a mistake on this topic is when the alleged victim (of, for example, harassment) is being interviewed. Oftentimes, the alleged victim seems credible and it is natural for the investigator to assume that the incident occurred as described. Moreover, the investigator wants to seem empathetic if the individual really is a victim. The investigator must not say anything to the complainant or anyone else, however, that suggests that they believe the allegations, because the allegations are precisely what is being investigated. The investigator can appear empathetic, yet unbiased, by declaring this dilemma up front to the complainant. For example, they can say something like: "I hope you understand my dilemma. I need to be neutral in order to determine what actually occurred. If you need help coping with this situation, I hope you will consider talking to our organization's Employee Assistance counselor."

7.1.4 Need for Interviewee Not to Discuss Investigation

The investigator should obtain an agreement with the interviewee as to what the interviewee will tell third parties about the interview and the subject matter of the investigation. Direct all employees not to discuss the investigation or interview with any other person and not to reveal the fact that they have been interviewed. Ask nonemployees to do the same. The investigation often involves a sensitive issue and the less discussion about the issue the better. Moreover, the integrity of the investigation suffers if individuals already interviewed discuss the subject with individuals whom have not yet been interviewed. The investigator wants everyone's unrehearsed responses to questions, not a group of employees collectively deciding upon a convenient revision of history.[1]

There are rare situations when the organization might want to conduct an open investigation in which it wants as many people as possible to know the subject matter of the investigation. For example, an investigation into drug use might send the message throughout the organization that deters such activity. Because an open investigation

---

[1]Employees will talk even if you instruct them not to, but this admonition typically reduces the extent of their conversations.

runs serious legal risks in most employment-related issues, do not conduct such an open investigation without consulting with legal counsel.

7.1.5 What Information Investigators Will Share

The investigator should advise the individual that the results of the investigation will be shared with a group of management who will review the issue and take action. The investigator also should assure the employee that he or she will attempt to limit the dissemination of the information provided, consistent with the needs of the investigation.

The investigator should not use the word confidential or confidentiality. This concept is vague and might be misunderstood. The interviewee often takes a promise of confidentiality as absolute. The investigator should never leave the interviewee with the false impression that they will keep the interviewee's identity or knowledge unknown to others within the organization. Indeed, many individuals outside the organization ultimately might learn exactly what the interviewee told the investigator, should it come to litigation.

The investigator should explain to each interviewee what they will later share with them what they can about the results of the investigation. Interviewees naturally will want to know "what happened." Unfortunately, most participants in the investigation should not receive any information about the organization's ultimate conclusions and actions taken, particularly disciplinary actions. Even with respect to alleged victims and wrongdoers, the investigator should not indicate at the outset how much information will be shared with them at the conclusion of your investigation.

7.1.6 Describe Investigation Process

The investigator should describe to the interviewee what will happen during the remainder of the investigative process. This necessarily will be vague. The investigator should simply state that he or she will be continuing with the investigation and might need to interview the individual again. Remind the individual not to discuss the subject matter of the interview with anyone else or the fact that they have been interviewed. The investigator should ask all interviewees to contact him or her if they remember or learn something after the interview. The investigator should provide interviewees with a convenient method of contacting him or her if they think of anything else related to the investigation.

7.1.7 No Promises as to Outcome

The investigator never should make any promise about what will happen after the investigation has been completed. The outcome of the investigation might be that the organization decides to take no action at all. If the investigator provides any indication about what will happen at the end of the investigation, they are leaving the impression that he or she has drawn conclusions about the situation without having all the facts. As discussed previously, this unnecessarily invites attacks to the integrity of the investigative process.

7.1.8 Organization Policies Involved

If applicable, the investigator should identify the organization's policy or policies involved. Frequently, this will involve asking interviewees if they have received a copy of the policy, whether they are familiar with it, etc. There are certain situations where the investigator might not want to divulge this up front, depending upon the interview strategy involved.

7.1.9 Seriousness of Issue

It is valuable to describe to interviewees that the organization is investigating a very serious issue. Again, depending upon the investigation strategy, the investigator might want to reveal that allegations of criminal wrongdoing have been made, that employees might lose their job if the allegations are proven, and so on.

7.1.10 Penalty for Providing False Information or Noncooperation

The investigator should let all interviewees know that that there is a severe penalty for providing false information or for not cooperating in the investigation. Employee interviewees should understand that if they provide false or misleading information to investigators, they could be subject to disciplinary action up to and including termination. It is important that the wrongdoer, as well as everyone else, understand the consequences of lying to investigators.

I recently conducted three investigations of senior management employees in a large financial organization. Each time, the underlying allegations were not so serious as to justify the manager's termination, even if the allegations were completely true. However, each time the manager lied to me during the course of the investigation (due to an arguably large ego). Because I had warned the managers that they could be terminated for lying during the investigation, and because I could prove that they lied to me, each manager was terminated.

It also is important to tell interviewees the consequences of their failure to cooperate. At this point, before any issue of noncooperation arises, the investigator should simply assert that the employee interviewee has a duty to cooperate.

7.1.11 Protection from Retaliation

It is critical that all interviewees understand that the organization will not retaliate against them for their participation in the investigation. The investigator should indicate to employees that they will not suffer any adverse consequences from organization management for their cooperation in the investigation. The investigator also should instruct all individuals interviewed to notify the investigator immediately if anyone takes any actions that they believe might be in retaliation for their involvement in the investigation. Similarly, the investigator should instruct all individuals interviewed to notify him or her immediately if they believe someone is attempting to interfere in any manner with the investigation.

7.1.12 Obtain Identity of Potential Witnesses

The investigator should ask interviewees for the identity of whom they believe might be a witness to any of the facts or others with whom the interviewee has discussed the subject matter of the investigation. At the beginning of the investigation, the investigator will not know all of the individuals who have relevant knowledge and must find out from interviewees who else might have helpful information. The investigator should ask about this at the beginning and end of the interview.

It also can be critical to learn with whom the interviewee has discussed the subject matter of the investigation. For example, often a victim of harassment does not immediately inform management about the situation, but confides in a friend or colleague. The fact that the victim discussed the incident soon after it happened might add to the victim's credibility.

7.1.13 Identify and/or Obtain Documents

At the outset of the interview process, the investigator will not possess all relevant documents. Written documents of one kind or another often provide valuable information. The investigator should ask all interviewees whether they have any memoranda, handwritten notes, electronic mail messages, or even voice mail messages that refer to or relate to the subject matter of the investigation. Similarly, ask all interviewees whether they sent to others any memoranda, handwritten notes, electronic mail messages, or voice mail messages that refer to or relate to the subject matter of the investigation. Collect the originals of such documents and give individuals a copy of the document if they wish to retain a copy.

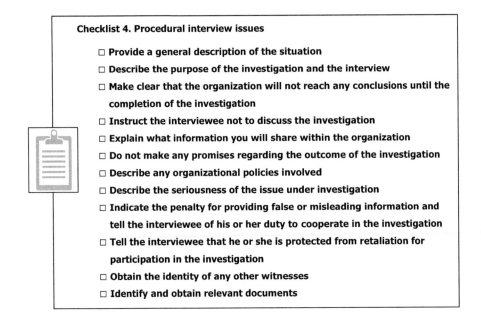

Checklist 4. Procedural interview issues

☐ Provide a general description of the situation

☐ Describe the purpose of the investigation and the interview

☐ Make clear that the organization will not reach any conclusions until the completion of the investigation

☐ Instruct the interviewee not to discuss the investigation

☐ Explain what information you will share within the organization

☐ Do not make any promises regarding the outcome of the investigation

☐ Describe any organizational policies involved

☐ Describe the seriousness of the issue under investigation

☐ Indicate the penalty for providing false or misleading information and tell the interviewee of his or her duty to cooperate in the investigation

☐ Tell the interviewee that he or she is protected from retaliation for participation in the investigation

☐ Obtain the identity of any other witnesses

☐ Identify and obtain relevant documents

7.2 ISSUES UNIQUE TO PUBLIC ENTITIES

Thus far, this guide has discussed issues common to all organizations. Although it is beyond the scope, there obviously are unique issues that will arise if the organization is a public entity. For example, many states have data practices statutes that restrict or govern access to certain data, data that the investigator might wish to obtain or, conversely, data that the investigator creates. The investigator in the public sector might find, for example, that certain individuals will seek access to the data collected about the complaint under investigation. Individuals typically will have access to certain data collected depending upon whether they are the alleged wrongdoer, the complainant, or a third party. The issue of what data is accessible to individuals is regulated by the data practices statute. If an individual seeks access to data obtained during the course of the investigation, the investigator should contact legal counsel immediately for an interpretation of the relevant law.

Although the data practices laws vary, certain generalizations can be made. Generally, personnel data collected during investigations is private (and inaccessible to third parties). However, the following information generally is public and accessible to third parties: (a) the existence and status of any complaints or charges against an employee or former employee; (b) whether the complaint or charge resulted in a disciplinary action; and (c) the final disposition of any disciplinary action together with the specific reasons for the action and data documenting the basis of the action, excluding data that would identify confidential sources who are public employees. The question of when a "final disposition" has occurred is a difficult legal question, and the investigator should not provide any of the above information to third parties without the approval and guidance of legal counsel.

Generally, an individual who is the subject of private or public data must be shown the data and, if desired, informed of the content and meaning of that data. It is conceivable that the alleged harasser and the complainant in a harassment investigation are both "subjects" of your investigative data. Again, the investigator should not provide any data to an alleged harasser or the complainant without the approval and guidance of legal counsel.

A special rule exists for alleged harassers in some states. The alleged harasser typically does not have access to data that would identify the complainant or other witnesses if the public entity determines that the alleged harasser's access to the data would (a) threaten the personal safety of the complainant or a witness, or (b) subject the complainant or witness to harassment. However, if a disciplinary proceeding is initiated against the alleged harasser, data on the complainant or witness typically must be made available to the employee as may be necessary for the alleged harasser to prepare for the proceeding. Again, the investigator should not make a decision about whether to provide any data to the alleged harasser without the approval and guidance of legal counsel.

7.3 SPECIFIC ISSUES

Unlike the above procedural issues, which arise in virtually all investigations, this section addresses certain specific issues that might or might not arise or be appropriate to discuss, depending upon the situation. There are a number of substantive issues to be aware of that can help you maximize the quantity and quality of information you receive during the investigation and minimize the legal risks inherent in this process.

7.3.1 Recording of Interviews

One question frequently asked is whether the investigator should record interviews. Certain statutes, for example, relating to police officers, requires the recording of interviews. Otherwise, recording generally is a bad idea.[2] Interviewees tend to be much more cautious and less forthcoming if they know their words are being recorded. Recording interviews also might give unnecessary weight to the investigation, thereby making it seem more serious than it really is. Sometimes, this can be harmful and misleading. If the organization has two interviewers, typically one can take detailed notes and both can testify about the interviewees' comments, so there should be little concern about the ability to later "prove" what the interviewee said.

Conversely, the investigator should consider asking interviewees if they are recording the interview. The investigator should advise interviewees that he or she is not recording the interview and that they are not permitted to do so either. If an individual has a recorder, make sure the recorder is removed from the room during the investigation.

If the individual insists upon recording the interview, your response depends upon whether the individual is an employee. If the individual is not an employee, you can only discourage the tape recording, ask for a copy of the tape recording, or choose not to interview the

---

[2]All too often, the recorded interview reveals flaws in the interview that the organization would just as soon not have memorialized. In my experience, recordings of interviews have hurt the party recording the interview just as frequently as they have helped. And that is true regardless of whether it is the company or the interviewee who has done the recording.

individual. Consult with legal counsel before permitting an individual to record the interview.

With respect to employees, the investigator may advise them that their management has directed them not to record the interview and that their failure to cooperate could subject them to discipline up to and including termination.

7.3.2 Presence of Attorneys or Third Parties

As a general rule, investigators should never conduct an interview with an attorney (or other third party such as a coworker) present. In the case of an attorney, this is true because the attorney (particularly the attorney of the alleged wrongdoer) might interfere with the conduct of the interview and might coach the individual in such a way that it is impossible to obtain candid, spontaneous answers. Moreover, this would unnecessarily permit the attorney to evaluate the interviewee, not to mention the investigator, as a witness. Finally, this sets a dangerous precedent that might lead to every interviewee requesting his or her personal attorney or a coworker is present for all sorts of occasions, such as important meetings or performance appraisals.

If the individual is not an employee, the investigator should evaluate how necessary it is to interview this individual and whether it makes sense to forego the interview if it must be in the attorney's or third party's presence. If the decision is made to proceed with the interview, the investigator should do so only with legal counsel present.

With respect to employees who want an attorney or other third party present, the investigator should tell them that this is unacceptable and that their management has directed them to cooperate in the interview without an attorney or third party present.

The investigator should review any exception to this rule with legal counsel. One exception that might make sense in an isolated situation is when the employee appears to be a vulnerable victim of, for example, harassment. *To repeat, if the investigator permits the presence of an employee's attorney, interview the employee only with the organization's attorney also present.*

Review the special situation of union environments discussed below.

7.3.3 Interviewing Nonemployees

The investigator should tell nonemployees that they are free to leave the interview at any time. To do otherwise is to expose the organization and the investigator unnecessarily to a legal claim of false imprisonment. If nonemployees indicate a desire to leave at any time during the interview, the investigator should state that they are free to leave but that their cooperation will be extremely valuable to the investigation and that it should not take up too much of their time.

In the event that a nonemployee is implicated and may be involved in the incident that necessitated the investigation, interviews of these individuals are critical to a successful resolution. A successful approach is to work with the management team from the nonemployee's company. It may be appropriate to have a manager from that company sit in during the interview of the nonemployee.

7.3.4 Requiring the Cooperation of Employees

The investigator may require employee cooperation. The investigator does not need to state up front to employees that they are free to leave. However, the investigator should tell employees who refuse to cooperate with the interview process that they are free to leave, but their management has directed them to cooperate with the investigation and that their failure to do so could subject them to disciplinary action up to and including termination. As an alternative to termination, management may advise employees who refuse to cooperate with the investigation that they are suspended without pay until they cooperate. The investigator should discuss this issue with management prior to the interviews.

7.3.5 Privacy Considerations

The investigator should be careful when asking questions about an individual's activities outside the workplace. In an attempt to evaluate a particular situation, interviewers often would like to obtain such information. However, questions about an individual's activities outside the workplace might be argued to invade the individual's privacy. For example, to evaluate whether an employee has sexually harassed another employee, it might be helpful to know about the individual's marital situation or sexual activities. But as stated, such questions might be argued to constitute an invasion of privacy.

Of course, the investigator may inquire into off-duty activities to the extent that they affect the workplace. For example, in certain circumstances the investigator may ask an employee about his or her off-duty conduct if an allegation has been made against that employee involving harassment that allegedly took place outside of work and is affecting an employee's work.

Given the legal risks of asking individuals about their activities outside the workplace, the investigator should review such questions in advance with legal counsel to ensure that the questions relate to the workplace and do not invade anyone's privacy unnecessarily.

7.3.6 Assume Attorney Involvement

The investigator always should assume the interviewee has an attorney. The investigator always should act as if the individuals being interviewed will replay the entire interview to their attorney (because often they do, sometimes literally). The investigator should not do or say anything that will give the individual's attorney an opportunity to allege that the investigator treated the individual unfairly.

7.3.7 Assume Verbatim Recording of Interviews

The investigator should conduct himself or herself as if there is a hidden video camera capturing the entire interview, including every word spoken. Many investigators have been embarrassed to find during the course of litigation that their interview was surreptitiously recorded and that they said something they regretted. Again, the investigator should not say or do anything that would be harmful to the organization if it were captured on camera.

Further, the investigator should assume that the entire interview will be repeated to a judge and jury. Some investigations will be challenged in litigation because the investigations frequently lead to employees losing their jobs or suffering other adverse employment consequences. The individual adversely affected by the organization's ultimate actions will be able to ask the investigator during a deposition under oath to state exactly what occurred during the interview (and during the entire investigative process). Ultimately, the investigator may have to testify in court about the interview and investigation. The investigator should not say or do anything that he or she would feel uncomfortable testifying about in front of a jury.

7.3.8 Discussion of Investigator Opinions and Conclusions

The investigator should not discuss his or her opinions or conclusions with any interviewees at any point during the investigation, for two reasons. First, the investigator does not want to give interviewees an indication of what answers he or she wants; the investigator wants to learn what information they have. Second, the investigator does not want to suggest that he or she has prejudged the facts. The investigator's conclusions should come at the *end* of the investigation and should be communicated only to the need-to-know group established at the outset of the investigation. If an interviewee can testify that the investigator stated a conclusion or opinion about the situation before the completion of the investigation, a jury might conclude that the investigation was biased.

7.3.9 Divulging Information Unnecessarily

The investigator should never divulge any more information than necessary to conduct the investigation. The less information the investigator divulges, the less likely interviewees will distribute that information to others including potential targets of the investigation. Moreover, this practice will reduce the risk of defamation claims. If the investigator divulges information to someone who does not have a need to know, and that information turns out to be false, anyone injured by the dissemination of the false information might bring a defamation claim.

The interviewer who avoids unnecessarily divulging information also asks the best questions. The best way to avoid divulging information unnecessarily is to begin with general questions and move to more specific questions. For example, if the investigation relates to whether John sexually harassed Mary, the investigator should not begin an interview with Sally by asking her whether she has seen John sexually harass Mary. Instead, the investigator should ask Sally whether she has observed or heard about any harassment in her work area. Let *Sally* be the one to bring up John's behavior if she has any relevant information about John. Ultimately, you might have to ask the specific question of whether you have seen John harass Mary, but if Sally brings it up first, the information will be more credible.

7.3.10 Assessing Demeanor

Nonverbal clues often can assist the investigator in evaluating an individual's credibility. The investigator should note long or frequent pauses, hesitance to answer certain questions, the interviewee's level of apparent preparation, body language, eye movements, and so on. Often, the investigator will end up with the proverbial "he said, she said" situation where there are no documents or witnesses to prove either side of an allegation. In these instances, the investigator often will need to make a credibility judgment, as opposed to just throwing up his or her hands and claiming that the facts are "inconclusive."[3] In these instances, the investigator will need to assess demeanor as part of an overall credibility judgment. Any observations about an interviewee's demeanor will support such a credibility judgment.

7.3.11 Avoiding Terms with Criminal Law Implications

The investigator should not use terms used by criminal investigators. The investigator should not use terms such as "suspect," "accused," "interrogation," "perpetrator," or "crime." The use of these terms unnecessarily increases the tension of the situation. Similarly, the investigator should not use these terms in the investigative notes. The investigator should use terms such as "alleged harasser," "complainant," "witness," "interviewee," "interviews," "questions," and "possible violation of organization policy."

> *Investigators with law enforcement backgrounds tend to use terms with criminal law implications more than others. Juries do not like these terms!*

7.3.12 Avoiding Terms with Legal Implications

Similarly, the investigator should not use phrases that suggest he or she is investigating violations of law, even if that is precisely what the investigator is doing. Let's again use the harassment example. If the investigator is looking into an allegation of sexual harassment, the organization of course wants to know if it has any legal liability as well as whether any organization policy has been violated. However, for purposes of what the interviewees hear, they need to know only

---

[3]Investigators sometimes think that the organization is legally protected by "inconclusive" determinations in these "he said, she said" situations. But the organization can get into just as much legal difficulty if a harasser does not receive discipline as when an alleged harasser wrongfully receives discipline.

that you are investigating a potential violation of organizational policy. This will not unnecessarily raise tensions and concerns.

More important, this distinction helps protect the organization legally. It is frequently, if not always, the case that an organization's policy is not identical to the law. Thus, the organization's policy against sexual harassment might be broader than the law and prohibit conduct that might be legal but that the organization wants to ban. Therefore, when an investigator concludes that someone violated the organization's policy, this does not automatically lead to a conclusion that the law has been violated.[4] If the investigator equates the two, the investigator is, in effect, making a legal judgment and handing a plaintiff's lawyer what is called an "admission" that the organization itself believed the law had been violated.

The investigator should make it clear that it is looking at potential policy violations, and should leave any legal conclusions to the organization's legal counsel.

7.3.13 Ask Open-Ended Questions, Then Press for Details

The investigator should avoid questions that the interviewee can answer yes or no. The investigator wants the interviewee to provide information, so he or she should ask questions that require lengthy, descriptive answers. The investigator should begin with open-ended questions like:

- What happened?
- Then what happened?
- Can you describe what she wore?
- Could you tell me exactly what she said?
- How did that make you feel?
- Could you list all the witnesses to that conversation?

Once the investigator has heard the interviewee provide general information about the various issues involved in the investigation, they must ask follow-up questions. The investigator never should accept

---

[4]This can get tricky. Sometimes the organization gets sued by both the alleged harassment victim and the alleged harasser, whom the organization terminates. If the alleged harasser sues for defamation, the damages certainly will be less if the organization does not have to concede that it accused that person of illegal conduct but merely a violation of organization policy.

generalities. One of the greatest failings of investigations is the lack of detailed information. For example, details are important to determine the severity of an allegation. For example, when Sally tells the investigator that she saw John "flirting" with Mary, it makes a big difference whether John was just winking at Mary or John had his hand on Mary's thigh. Questions like the following can elicit more precise details after an individual makes a general comment:

- What exactly happened?
- Tell me more about that incident?
- What do you mean by that?
- What exactly did he (or she) say?
- When did this occur?
- Where did this occur?
- Were there any witnesses?
- Who made the statement?
- How did he (or she) act?
- What did you see, specifically?

Details are important to corroborate or disprove allegations. An individual who has only a vague recollection of an event normally is not as credible as an individual who can recall specific details of the event. This is particularly true if the investigator can corroborate any of the details. Details are important to obtain because they are helpful to refresh the recollection of witnesses to an event. For example, an individual might not recall whether she saw anyone "flirting" but might recall seeing someone placing his hand on a coworker's thigh.

7.3.14 Hearsay and Rumor

Often, individuals will make statements that suggest that they have firsthand knowledge of facts, when in fact they are merely repeating a rumor or other statement that someone else made to them. It is valuable to know what the rumors are about an individual or a situation, but it is even more important to know whether an individual's statement is based upon rumor or personal knowledge. For example, if Sally states that John is always making derogatory comments about women, the investigator should ask Sally how she knows that. The investigator should ask Sally if she personally has heard John make such remarks. If Sally has not heard these remarks personally, find out why Sally believes John has made these remarks. It is hard work, but the investigator should identify hearsay and rumor as such, and then see if the hearsay or rumor can be tracked back to someone with personal knowledge. Personal knowledge, of course, is far more valuable in determining what actually occurred than hearsay or rumor.

Checklist 5. Technical interview issues

- ☐ Make sure the interviewee is not recording the interview
- ☐ Do not allow the interviewee to have an attorney present without consulting first with legal counsel
- ☐ Nonemployees have a right not to participate in and to terminate any interview
- ☐ The organization may require the cooperation of its employees in the investigation and interview process
- ☐ Be careful not to invade the privacy of any individual
- ☐ Assume that all parties are represented by and getting advice from an attorney
- ☐ Assume that a verbatim recording of every interview will exist
- ☐ Do not discuss your opinions or conclusions with any interviewee and do not discuss your opinions or conclusions until you have completed the investigation
- ☐ Do not divulge any information to interviewees unnecessarily
- ☐ Assess demeanor of interviewees as part of overall credibility assessment
- ☐ Avoid terms with criminal law implications
- ☐ Avoid an appearance that you are investigating a violation of law or making legal judgments
- ☐ Ask open-ended questions, then press for details
- ☐ Identify hearsay and rumor

7.4 STYLE ISSUES

7.4.1 Professionalism

The investigator must act professionally at all times. Again, the test is whether the investigator would be proud of his or her conduct if it were replayed on video to a judge or jury. The investigator should never lose his temper. The investigator should never argue with the interviewee. If the interviewee starts asking the investigator questions that are not appropriate to answer, the investigator should politely state that the organization will not permit him or her to answer those questions and that his or her role is to ask the questions and the interviewee's role is to provide information helpful to the investigation if the interviewee possesses it.

7.4.2 Objectivity

The investigator must never appear to be biased or to have prejudged the outcome of the investigation. When interviewing alleged victims, the investigator should be sympathetic without appearing to prematurely accept their claims as true. This is a difficult task, but the investigator cannot appear to believe the victim prior to the completion of the investigation. Imagine the problems this would create if the investigator ultimately concludes that the wrongdoing did not occur and the victim was not telling the truth. Imagine the attack upon the investigation that would occur if the alleged wrongdoer learns that the investigator was siding with the complainant before the completion of the investigation. Objectivity and open-mindedness are critical components of any good investigation.

7.4.3 Listening

The investigator should use active listening skills by, for example, rephrasing what the interviewee said to see if the investigator heard or interpreted the interviewee correctly.

7.4.4 Building Trust

The investigator can build trust with the interviewee by doing all of the things discussed in these materials. Acting professionally, appearing objective, and listening closely to interviewees will give them confidence that the investigator knows what he or she is doing and is not on a witch hunt. The investigator should emphasize his or her impartiality and desire to do the right thing. Whenever possible, the investigator should emphasize that he or she is not the decision-maker, simply the gatherer of facts.

7.5 ISSUES UNIQUE TO THE SUBJECT MATTER

In addition to all the other issues that the investigator must master, every investigation entails issues unique to the subject matter of that investigation. For example, a workplace violence investigation will involve numerous critical substantive and procedural issues not involved in most other investigations. Similarly, a sexual harassment investigation will require the investigator to understand numerous issues unique to that subject matter.

Following are descriptions of additional unique issues that the investigator must address during a sexual harassment investigation.

7.5.1 Determine Whether a Violation of the Organization's Policy Has Occurred

The investigator needs to keep in mind that he or she is attempting to determine whether the organization's policy (e.g., offensive behavior or harassment policy) has been violated, not whether there has been sexual or other harassment as legally defined. The investigator needs to keep this distinction in mind and never accuse an alleged harasser of violating the law, but only address whether the alleged harasser has violated an organization policy. Whether an alleged harasser has violated the law calls for a legal conclusion, which the investigator should not be making. For example, the organization policy's definition of sexual harassment is probably broader than the legal definition, so it is quite possible that an individual could violate the organization's policy without engaging in illegal sexual harassment. To accuse someone of committing "sexual harassment" as defined by the law when all he or she really did was violate a broader harassment policy could lead the accused to bring a defamation claim.

7.5.2 Determine Whether the Complainant Made a Contemporaneous Complaint

The investigator obviously must study the organization's policy that he or she is investigating. A typical sexual harassment policy, for example, might adopt the legal requirement that the conduct must be unwelcome to the target of the conduct in order to qualify as prohibited sexual harassment. One valuable piece of evidence in determining whether sexual conduct was unwelcome is if the complainant made a contemporaneous complaint or protest about the alleged harasser's conduct. This complaint is not necessarily the original that was made to the organization. Therefore, the investigator should ask the complainant if he or she complained to anyone about the alleged harasser's conduct. This could be a complaint to the alleged harasser, a family member, coworker, or a nonemployee. The investigator should find out when the complaints occurred. Then the investigator should seek to verify the complainant's claims by asking witnesses if they ever heard the complainant complain or protest about the alleged harasser's conduct. If the complainant made no contemporaneous complaint, find out why not. Many victims of harassment may fear repercussions from complaining about the harassment and that fear might explain a delay in opposing the conduct.

7.5.3 Examine the Complainant's Conduct as well as That of the Alleged Harasser

Similarly, it is important in determining the welcomeness of the sexual conduct to examine the actions of the complainant. Many court cases have held that a complainant has welcomed sexual conduct by acting in a sexually aggressive manner, using sexually-oriented language, or soliciting the sexual conduct. On the other hand, occasional use of sexually explicit language does not necessarily suggest that the alleged harasser's sexual conduct was welcome. The investigator should not ask the complainant general questions about past sexual conduct. Any past conduct of the complainant must relate to the alleged harasser.

7.5.4 Determine Whether a Hostile Work Environment Exists

One of the most difficult tasks the organization will face in a harassment investigation is determining whether the facts suggest that a hostile work environment exists, because these determinations must be based upon the totality of circumstances and will vary from case to case. However, the investigator's job during the fact-finding phase is to gather the information necessary for this determination. The investigator should look at:

a. Whether the conduct was verbal or physical.
b. How frequently it was repeated.
c. Whether the conduct was hostile and patently offensive.
d. Whether the alleged harasser was a coworker or supervisor.
e. Whether others joined in perpetrating the harassment.
f. Whether the harassment was directed at more than one individual.
g. The effect of the harassment on the complainant.

This section is for illustrative purposes only. It is intended to demonstrate that every type of investigation will require a substantive understanding of issues beyond general investigative techniques. To the extent that the investigator is unfamiliar with those substantive issues, the investigator should do his or her homework before commencing the investigation.

Also, although the investigator is not making legal conclusions or suggesting to interviewees that he or she is looking at potential violations of law, the reality is that legal counsel will review (if not directly) many of these investigations and will rely upon the facts that the investigations develop to give legal advice to the organization. Therefore, it is critical that the investigator understand the legal claims related to the subject matter of the investigation. An investigator can and should investigate factual questions relevant to a legal claim.

Taking Notes

8.1 DESIGNATE A PRIMARY NOTE TAKER 51

8.2 WHAT TO INCLUDE IN NOTES 51

8.3 NEED FOR COMPLETENESS 51

8.4 EXCLUDE INTERPRETATION, SUBJECTIVE COMMENTS OR CONCLUSIONS 52

8.5 NOTE DEMEANOR 52

8.6 WRITE FOR THE JURY 52

The most lasting and important evidence to defend the investigation conducted is the notes the investigator has taken during the investigation. The following suggestions will help investigators improve the quality of their note taking.

8.1 DESIGNATE A PRIMARY NOTE TAKER

As stated in section six, the investigator should conduct the interviews with one other interviewer if possible. One investigator should be the primary note taker, concentrating on taking complete and accurate notes. The other investigator can concentrate on asking questions.

8.2 WHAT TO INCLUDE IN NOTES

The investigator's notes of each interview always should contain:

1. Date of interview
2. Location of interview
3. Names of those present
4. Starting and ending times of interview

8.3 NEED FOR COMPLETENESS

The notes should identify the speaker making the statement, use the exact words of the speaker whenever possible, and be written so that someone else can pick them up and read and understand them. As soon as the interview is completed, the investigator should go through the notes and fill in any information that he or she wants to capture that could not be written down during the course of the interview.

8.4 EXCLUDE INTERPRETATION, SUBJECTIVE COMMENTS OR CONCLUSIONS

The investigator should not put his or her interpretations or subjective comments or thoughts in the investigative notes. Such comments will be attacked as evidence that the investigator was biased or had made up his or her mind before completing the investigation. The investigator should save subjective comments until he or she is done with the investigation and give those comments orally to the need-to-know group.

8.5 NOTE DEMEANOR

The investigator should note the demeanor of the interviewees. An individual's demeanor is objective behavior that can be documented. Although the investigator should not record subjective conclusions, he or she should record observable behavior. The investigator should put down in writing such things as:

1. Body language
2. Frequent or long pauses
3. Eye movement
4. Hesitance to answer certain questions
5. Level of apparent preparation
6. Voice inflections, for example, loudness

8.6 WRITE FOR THE JURY

The investigator's notes will, in almost all circumstances, be discoverable to a plaintiff and might be evidence at a trial. The investigator should assume this. Clear interview notes will permit a jury to understand exactly what information the organization had when it made the decision being challenged.

Checklist 6. Taking notes

- ☐ Designate a primary note taker
- ☐ Include date, location, time started and stopped, and identification of those present
- ☐ Make sure notes are complete and fill in information immediately after interview
- ☐ Exclude interpretation, subjective comments and conclusions
- ☐ Write down objective evidence of demeanor
- ☐ Always write for the jury

Taking Written Statements

9.1 OBTAINING VOLUNTARY STATEMENTS 55
9.2 REQUIRING EMPLOYEE STATEMENTS.. 55
9.3 IDENTIFY TOPICS BUT NOT CONTENT... 56
9.4 ELEMENTS OF THE STATEMENT 56

As discussed in section six, there are many good reasons to take statements from the individuals interviewed. Before taking written statements, investigators should obtain the approval and guidance of legal counsel. If the investigator is going to take statements, he or she should follow these guidelines.

9.1 OBTAINING VOLUNTARY STATEMENTS

The investigator should ask individuals if they will assist the investigation by providing a written statement. The investigator should explain that a written statement would reduce the chance of the individual being misinterpreted or misquoted. A written statement also would help individuals provide a consistent response if later asked about the same issue. Of course, the investigator may not require nonemployees to provide statements.

9.2 REQUIRING EMPLOYEE STATEMENTS

The investigator may require employees to provide a written statement. If the investigator is unable to persuade an employee to provide a voluntary statement, the investigator may advise the employee that the organization's management has directed the employee to provide a statement and that the employee's refusal to cooperate could subject him or her to discipline up to and including termination. How to address an employee who refuses to cooperate or provide a written statement should be discussed with the employee's manager prior to the interview.

9.3 IDENTIFY TOPICS BUT NOT CONTENT

Although the investigator may require employees to provide statements, under no circumstances should the investigator attempt to influence what any individual places in the statement. The investigator may, however, advise individuals (and require employees) to cover certain topics in their statement. For example, the investigator never should tell an individual to write "the light was green," but may advise the individual (and require the employee) to include in the statement the color of the light.

9.4 ELEMENTS OF THE STATEMENT

If the individual is voluntarily providing a statement, the following paragraph should be dictated to the individual as the first paragraph of the statement:

> I [name] provide the following voluntary statement to [name] who has identified himself [or herself] as [title]. This statement is provided without coercion, or receipt or promise of reward and is unconditionally submitted.

If the employee is not providing the statement voluntarily, the following paragraph should be the first paragraph of the statement:

> I [name] provide the following statement to [name] who has identified himself [or herself] as [title].

After the first paragraph is completed, the investigator should instruct individuals to tell their story, making sure to include the necessary who, what, why, when, where, and how information. This part of the statement should not be dictated to them, but the investigator should guide them to make sure that they cover all pertinent topics.

The investigator should follow these procedures:

1. Individuals should hand write or print their statement, unless their handwriting is illegible.
2. Instruct the individual to include a statement start and finish time at the top of the first page.
3. Instruct the individual not to skip lines.
4. Instruct the individual to sign, date, and number each page of the statement in the top margin.
5. Instruct the individual to initial any cross-outs or erasures.

6. At the conclusion of the statement, have the individual write:

I have read the foregoing consisting of this and (number) other pages. I have initialed each page and all corrections and deletions. This statement is true and correct to the best of my knowledge.

Have the individual write *End of Statement* and sign the document.
7. The statement should be witnessed by at least one person, preferably two.
8. Both witnesses should sign and date every page of the statement.
9. Provide a copy of the statement to the individual upon completion.

Checklist 7. Taking written statements

☐ **Seek voluntary statements**

☐ **Employees may be required to provide statements**

☐ **Identify the topics the individual should discuss in the statement, but not the content**

☐ **Statements should:**

- **Include statement of voluntariness when appropriate**
- **Discuss all pertinent topics**
- **Be handwritten**
- **Include a start and finish time at top of first page**
- **Not skip lines**
- **Have all cross-outs or erasures initialed**
- **Have a concluding statement**
- **Be witnessed by at least one person**
- **Have signature and date of witnesses on every page**
- **Be provided to individual upon completion (copy)**

Reporting Findings

10.1 REPORTING PRELIMINARY CONCLUSIONS 59

10.2 INCLUSION OF ATTORNEY 60

10.3 REPORTING CONCLUSIONS, RECOMMENDATIONS 60

**10.4 AFTER CONSENSUS IS REACHED, CREATE A
SUMMARY REPORT** 61

10.5 COMMUNICATION BEYOND THE NEED-TO-KNOW GROUP 61

10.6 ATTORNEY FILE REVIEW 61

10.1 REPORTING PRELIMINARY CONCLUSIONS

If the investigator communicates in writing any preliminary impressions prior to a meeting of the need-to-know group, those impressions, conclusions, or recommendations about the investigation should be directed to legal counsel. The communication should have the following heading at the top: "Attorney–Client Privileged Communication." The communication should begin with the words, "As you requested, the following sets forth my impressions, conclusions and recommendations that might assist you in forming your legal opinion as to how we should resolve the issues involved in this investigation." This will best protect the claim of attorney–client privilege, permitting the organization not to reveal the preliminary conclusions to an employee suing the organization.

The protection of the attorney–client privilege is particularly valuable when there are differences of opinion about the appropriate course of action at the preliminary stage. Once, a human resources manager investigating a complaint sent an email to his boss near the conclusion of the investigation opining that the alleged harasser be fired. This email was not protected by the attorney–client privilege. The rest of the organization, including legal counsel, was unaware of this email. The ultimate conclusion was to give this harasser a slap on the wrist. Later, the victim sued the organization and this email was discovered. Imagine the problems created when it was revealed that the organization did not follow the advice of the investigator and human resources manager!

Of course, the attorney—client privilege is also valuable when the investigation yields information tending to prove that the organization has legal liability. Handing over the investigative report to the plaintiffs' lawyers during discovery would make it that much easier for plaintiffs to prove their case.

10.2 INCLUSION OF ATTORNEY

After the investigator has completed any significant investigation but hopefully before he or she has put any conclusions in writing, a meeting of the need-to-know group should be held to discuss the preliminary investigation findings (including the investigator's impressions, conclusions, and recommendations). This meeting should include the organization's legal counsel so that the organization can take advantage of the attorney-client privilege. The purpose of this meeting is so that the need-to-know group can hear the investigative findings, determine if further investigation is warranted, determine if any organization policy has been violated, and determine what discipline or other action, if any, is warranted. It also is possible that, in conjunction with legal counsel, the group will look at whether any laws have been violated.

It is important that the need-to-know group reach a consensus on what action to take, because disagreement on the appropriate action can be devastating if the actual action taken is later challenged. For example, some individual might lobby for terminating an alleged harasser prior to the meeting of the need-to-know group yet the group might end up deciding not to terminate the alleged harasser. If the alleged harassment victim later sues and discovers that someone was lobbying to fire the alleged harasser but the company ignored that person's opinion, the alleged victim's lawyer would have some valuable ammunition.

10.3 REPORTING CONCLUSIONS, RECOMMENDATIONS

The investigator should make his or her written findings available to others in management first by asking legal counsel to share the report with the need-to-know group. Again, it is best to communicate the preliminary investigation findings orally in a meeting including legal counsel. However, if the investigator must provide a written report before a meeting as described above, he or she should only give one to the organization's legal counsel. The legal counsel can, in turn, provide the findings to others in management while providing legal advice to the group, protecting the findings as well as the legal advice from disclosure because of the attorney-client privilege.

10.4 AFTER CONSENSUS IS REACHED, CREATE A SUMMARY REPORT

After a consensus is reached among the need-to-know group as to the proper course of action, the investigator should create a written summary report of the investigation. This report should include the following items:

1. A statement of the complaint
2. A summary of the investigation conducted
3. The factual findings of the investigation, including resolution of conflicting statements and credibility assessments
4. Identification of behaviors, actions, or statements that violate the organization's policies
5. Disciplinary or other action taken

10.5 COMMUNICATION BEYOND THE NEED-TO-KNOW GROUP

The organization, in consultation with legal counsel, should determine what information to communicate to individuals beyond the need-to-know group (established prior to the start of the investigation). There are some circumstances in which it is appropriate to reveal conclusions or other information about the investigation to a victim or to an individual accused of wrongdoing. There are few circumstances in which it is appropriate to reveal information learned during the investigation to other participants in the investigation, other employees, or nonemployees.

10.6 ATTORNEY FILE REVIEW

Ideally, legal counsel should review the investigative file after completion of the investigation. This will give the attorney an opportunity to ensure that the file does not contain any ambiguous or inappropriate information. The organization also should determine where the investigation file should be kept for safekeeping and what information, if any, should be placed in any employee personnel file.

Checklist 8. Reporting findings

☐ Avoid putting preliminary conclusions in writing, but any preliminary conclusions should be sent to legal counsel for the purpose of obtaining legal advice

☐ Convene a meeting of the need-to-know group and include legal counsel

☐ If others need to see preliminary conclusions, ask legal counsel to send out those conclusions as part of an attorney–client privileged communication

☐ After the need-to-know group meeting has developed a consensus, create a summary report of the investigation

☐ Do not communicate any investigation results beyond the need-to-know group except with the advice of legal counsel

☐ Have legal counsel review the investigation file once the investigation is over

Investigations in Union Environments

11.1 HANDLING THE PRESS... **63**
11.2 CONCLUSION... **64**

Investigators should consult with legal counsel prior to conducting investigations in a union environment to determine if any of the investigative practices described in earlier sections would violate the terms of any collective bargaining agreement, labor laws, or labor relations practices.

For example, some union employees will ask to have their union representative present during an interview. If the interviewee is a target of the investigation or otherwise might be subject to discipline, that interviewee might have the right to have a union representative present during the interview. Even if the individual would not be subject to discipline (e.g., a witness not implicated any way in wrongdoing), the organization might conclude that it is desirable as a matter of policy that such an individual may have a union representative present during the interview. The union representative may not, however, interfere with the interview. If the investigator feels that a union representative is interfering with an interview, the investigator should immediately contact legal counsel for advice as to how to proceed.

11.1 HANDLING THE PRESS

The investigator's job is hard enough without asking him or her to deal with the press. Before any investigation, the investigator should be aware of the organization's public relations representative or contact person and refer any press inquiries to that person. If the investigator has to assume any responsibility for press contacts, he or she should contact legal counsel for a discussion of do-s and don'ts *before* the press calls. If the investigator has not thought in advance about how to respond to the press, it is too late to start thinking about when the call comes in.

11.2 CONCLUSION

It is impossible to analyze all of the issues that an investigator will confront while conducting investigations in the employment setting. However, the best practices and tips provided in this guide provide a framework for investigators in the planning and execution of a successful investigation. The goal of the investigator should always be to implement an investigative strategy that will maximize the information obtained while minimizing legal exposure for the organization.

Checklists

1. IDENTIFYING INVESTIGATORS

☐ Are special skills required?
☐ Should an attorney conduct the investigation?
☐ Are there actual or potential conflicts of interest that should be addressed?
☐ Are the proposed investigators objective and resistant to pressure?
☐ Will any party claim the proposed investigators are biased?
☐ Are the proposed investigators the individuals who can maximize the information obtained in interviews?

2. OBTAINING DOCUMENTS

☐ Personnel files
☐ Telephone records
☐ Expense account records
☐ Personnel information on computer
☐ Appointment calendars
☐ Time cards
☐ Building entrance/exit records
☐ Computer/word processing disks (and hard drive memory)
☐ Electronic mail records
☐ Voice mail records

3. PLANNING THE INVESTIGATION

☐ Minimize witness intimidation
☐ Form investigative team and divide duties
☐ Establish a time frame for completion of the investigation
☐ Prepare confirmatory memorandum to complainant
☐ Obtain and review relevant documents
☐ Consider special investigative techniques
☐ Identify interviewees
☐ Establish an interview location

- ☐ Arrange interview order
- ☐ Prepare opening and closing comments
- ☐ Prepare set of written interview questions
- ☐ Plan for multiple interviews
- ☐ Decide whether to obtain written statements
- ☐ Take detailed notes of investigation planning process

4. PROCEDURAL INTERVIEW ISSUES

- ☐ Provide a general description of the situation
- ☐ Describe the purpose of the investigation and the interview
- ☐ Make clear that the organization will not reach any conclusions until the completion of the investigation
- ☐ Instruct the interviewee not to discuss the investigation
- ☐ Explain what information you will share within the organization
- ☐ Do not make any promise regarding the outcome of the investigation
- ☐ Describe any organizational policies involved
- ☐ Describe the seriousness of the issue under investigation
- ☐ Indicate the penalty for providing false or misleading information and tell the interviewee of his or her duty to cooperate in the investigation
- ☐ Tell the interviewee he or she is protected from retaliation for participation in the investigation
- ☐ Obtain the identity of any other witnesses
- ☐ Identify and obtain relevant documents

5. TECHNICAL INTERVIEW ISSUES

- ☐ Make sure the interviewee is not recording the interview
- ☐ Do not allow the interviewee to have an attorney present without consulting first with legal counsel
- ☐ Nonemployees have a right not to participate in and to terminate any interview
- ☐ The organization may require the cooperation of its employees in the investigation and interview process
- ☐ Be careful not to invade the privacy of any individual
- ☐ Assume that all parties are represented by and getting advice from an attorney
- ☐ Assume that a verbatim recording of every interview will exist

- ☐ Do not discuss your opinions or conclusions with any interviewee and do not discuss your opinions or conclusions until you have completed the investigation
- ☐ Do not divulge any information to interviewees unnecessarily
- ☐ Assess demeanor of interviewees as part of overall credibility assessment
- ☐ Avoid terms with criminal law implications
- ☐ Avoid an appearance that you are investigating a violation of law or making legal judgments
- ☐ Ask open-ended questions; then press for details
- ☐ Identify hearsay and rumor

6. TAKING NOTES

- ☐ Designate a primary note taker
- ☐ Include date, location, time started and stopped, and identification of those present
- ☐ Make sure notes are complete and fill in information immediately after interview
- ☐ Exclude interpretation, subjective comments, and conclusions
- ☐ Write down objective evidence of demeanor
- ☐ Always write for the jury

7. TAKING WRITTEN STATEMENTS

- ☐ Seek voluntary statements
- ☐ You may require employees to provide statements
- ☐ Identify the topics the individual should discuss in the statement, but not the content
- ☐ Statements should:
  - Include statement of voluntariness when appropriate
  - Discuss all pertinent topics
  - Be handwritten
  - Include a start and finish time at top of first page
  - Not skip lines
  - Have all cross-outs or erasures initialed
  - Have a concluding statement
  - Be witnessed by at least one person
  - Have signature and date of witnesses on every page
  - Be provided to individual upon completion (copy)

8. REPORTING FINDINGS

☐ Avoid putting preliminary conclusions in writing, but any preliminary conclusions should be sent to legal counsel for the purpose of obtaining legal advice

☐ Convene a meeting of the need-to-know group and include legal counsel

☐ If others need to see preliminary conclusions, ask legal counsel to send out those conclusions as part of an attorney–client privileged communication

☐ After the need-to-know group meeting has developed a consensus, create a summary report of the investigation

☐ Do not communicate any investigation results beyond the need-to-know group except with the advice of legal counsel

☐ Have legal counsel review the investigation file once the investigation is over

9. WHAT NOT TO DO

☐ Do not ignore an "informal" complaint

☐ Do not assume you will remember the case later—record it!

☐ Do not skip over opening and closing statements during the interview

☐ Never assume innocence or guilt

☐ Avoid terms with criminal law implications

☐ Do not ask "yes" or "no" questions

☐ Don't assume you can do it all—know when to seek professional help

Sample Confirmation Memorandum

CONFIDENTIAL

To: Employee

From: Investigator

Date:

Re: Our conversation of [date]

This memo is to confirm the issues you raised in our meeting/ discussion of [date]. As I understand from our discussion, you feel inappropriate comments/actions have been made to or directed at you at work. The facts you related to me are:

[list in detail]

If I have missed or misunderstood something that you told me, or if you have any additional concerns or facts, please let me know immediately. I have informed you that [name of investigator] will conduct a thorough and fair investigation.

I also reviewed with you the general roadmap of the investigation. [Name of investigator] will review the information [and documents] you provided to me. [Name of investigator] will gather facts from other sources, including employee interviews, to assist in resolving this concern. [Name of investigator] will keep you informed of the progress of the investigation.

We also discussed the expectations that the organization has of you. **You** agreed to:

- Fully cooperate with the investigation;
- Honestly answer all questions; and
- Provide all **information/documents** that you believe may help me review and address your concern.

You also agreed that **you** would not discuss this investigation with anyone who does not have a legitimate need to know. **If you have any questions about anything set forth in this memo, or if you have any additional information to provide, please contact [name of investigator] at [phone number].**

Investigation Matrix

In the following pages, checklists, notes, and documentation reminders are consolidated in one spreadsheet. One should be used for each investigation.

Investigation Matrix • *Never ignore an "informal" complaint* • *Do not assume you'll remember a case later—Document It!* • *Know when to seek professional help*

Name of Investigation:	Date:	Estimated Timeframe for Completion:
Identifying Investigators (Section V)	**Investigative Team Names / Titles / Duties**	
Form investigative team and divide duties.	1. _____ 2. _____ 3. _____ 4. _____ 5. _____	
☐ 1. Special skills required?	Notes:	
☐ 2. Should attorney conduct investigation?	Notes:	
☐ 3. Are there actual/potential conflicts of interest that should be addressed?	Notes:	
☐ 4. Are proposed investigators objective & resistant to pressure?	Notes:	
☐ 5. Will anyone claim proposed investigators are biased?	Notes:	
☐ 6. Can proposed investigators maximize information obtained in interviews?	Notes:	
Documents (Section VI E) Obtain and review relevant documents	☐ Personnel hard copy files ☐ Telephone records ☐ Expense account records ☐ Personnel files on computer	☐ Appointment calendars ☐ Time cards ☐ Building entrance/exit records	☐ Computer/word processing disks (and hard drive memory) ☐ Electronic mail records ☐ Voice mail records

Planning the Investigation (Section VI)	Identify Interviewees (Section VI G) Plan for multiple interviews	Interview Order	Interview Issues: Procedural (Section VII A)
☐ Prepare confirmatory memo to complainant (See Appendix B for sample)	1.	☐	☐ Minimize witness intimidation
☐ Establish interview location	2.	☐	☐ Provide a general description of the situation
☐ Consider special investigative techniques	3.	☐	☐ Describe the purpose of the investigator and the interview
	4.	☐	☐ Make clear that the organization will not reach any conclusions until the completion of the investigation
	5.	☐	☐ Obtain the identity of any other witnesses
☐ Prepare opening and closing statements	6.	☐	☐ Instruct the interviewee not to discuss the investigation
	7.	☐	☐ Explain what information you will share within the organization
	8.	☐	
☐ Decide whether to obtain written statements	9.	☐	☐ Do not make any promise regarding the outcome of the investigation
	10.	☐	☐ Describe any organizational policies involved
	11.	☐	
☐ Keep detailed notes of planning process	12.	☐	☐ Describe the seriousness of the issue under investigation

Interview Issues: Procedural (Section VII A)

☐ Indicate the penalty for providing false or misleading information and tell the interviewee of his or her duty to cooperate in the investigation

☐ Tell the interviewee he or she is protected from retaliation for participation in the investigation

☐ Obtain the identity of any other witnesses

☐ Identify and obtain relevant documents

IMPORTANT

✓ Do not skip over opening and closing statements during the interview

✓ Never assume innocence or guilt

✓ Avoid terms with criminal law implications

✓ Do not ask "yes" or "no" questions

Notes:

Interview Issues: Specific (Section VII C)

☐ Make sure the interviewee is not recording the interview

☐ Do not allow the interviewee to have an attorney present without consulting first with legal counsel

☐ Non-employees have a right not to participate in and to terminate any interview

☐ The organization may require the cooperation of its employees in the investigation and interview process

☐ Be careful not to invade the privacy of any individual

☐ Assume that all parties are represented by, and getting advice from, an attorney

☐ Assume that a verbatim recording of every interview will exist

☐ Do not discuss your opinions or conclusions with any interviewee and do not discuss your opinions or conclusions until you have completed the investigation

☐ Do not divulge any information to interviewees unnecessarily

☐ Assess demeanor of interviewees as part of overall credibility assessment

☐ Avoid terms with criminal law implications

☐ Avoid the appearance you are investigating a violation of law or making legal judgments

☐ Ask open-ended questions, then press for details

☐ Identify hearsay and rumor

Taking Notes (Section VIII)

- Designate a primary note taker
- Include date, location, time started and stopped, and identification of those present
- Make sure notes are complete and fill in information immediately after interview
- Exclude interpretation, subjective comments and conclusions
- Write down objective evidence of demeanor
- Always write for the jury

Taking Written Statements (Section IX)

- Seek voluntary statements
- You may require employees to provide statements
- Identify the topics the individual should discuss in the statement, but not the content
- Statements should:

  ☐ Include statement of voluntariness when appropriate

  ☐ Discuss all pertinent topics

  ☐ Be handwritten

  ☐ Include a start and finish time at top of first page

  ☐ Not skip lines

  ☐ Have all cross-outs or erasures initialed

  ☐ Have a concluding statement

  ☐ Be witnessed by at least one person

  ☐ Have signature and date of witnesses on every page

  ☐ Be provided to individual upon completion (copy)

Reporting Findings (Section X)

☐ Avoid putting preliminary conclusions in writing, but any preliminary conclusions should be sent to legal counsel for the purpose of obtaining legal advice

☐ Convene a meeting of the need-to-know group and include legal counsel

☐ If others need to see preliminary conclusions, ask legal counsel to send out those conclusions as part of an attorney–client privileged communication

☐ After the need-to-know group meeting has developed a consensus, create a summary report of the investigation

☐ Do not communicate any investigation results beyond the need-to-know group except with the advice of legal counsel

☐ Have legal counsel review the investigation file when the investigation is over

Case Notes:

With over 22 years of experience addressing security matters from prevention and counseling to training and litigation, John D. Thompson is a nationally-recognized expert in the area of workplace violence. He has provided consulting, counseling, training, and litigation services to the government and to numerous Fortune 500 and other companies for workplace violence and related security problems. Consistently included on the "Best Lawyers in America" list, John has developed workplace violence training programs and videotapes for supervisors and managers and has tried a workplace homicide lawsuit to jury verdict. Also a member of the Security Executive Council Content Expert Faculty, John helps develop strategic security services and products for Council members.

Currently a partner with the Minneapolis law firm of Oberman Thompson, LLC, John formerly served as in-house counsel for 3M Company where he advised the human resources, employee assistance, medical, and security departments. John participated in the development of 3M's progressive and proactive approach to the problem of workplace violence, including incident management and the development of a threat assessment team and other preventive techniques.

He enjoys a unique career combination: that of practicing attorney and corporate development of employer workplace violence management and security programs. He holds both B.A. and J.D. degrees with honors from Georgetown University.

About Elsevier's Security Executive Council Risk Management Portfolio

Elsevier's Security Executive Council Risk Management Portfolio is the voice of the security leader. It equips executives, practitioners, and educators with research-based, proven information and practical solutions for successful security and risk management programs. This portfolio covers topics in the areas of risk mitigation and assessment, ideation and implementation, and professional development. It brings trusted operational research, risk management advice, tactics, and tools to business professionals. Previously available only to the Security Executive Council community, this content—covering corporate security, enterprise crisis management, global IT security, and more—provides real-world solutions and "how-to" applications. This portfolio enables business and security executives, security practitioners, and educators to implement new physical and digital risk management strategies and build successful security and risk management programs.

Elsevier's Security Executive Council Risk Management Portfolio is a key part of the **Elsevier Risk Management & Security Collection**. The collection provides a complete portfolio of titles for the business executive, practitioner, and educator by bringing together the best imprints in risk management, security leadership, digital forensics, IT security, physical security, homeland security, and emergency management: Syngress, which provides cutting-edge computer and information security material; Butterworth-Heinemann, the premier security, risk management, homeland security, and disaster-preparedness publisher; and Anderson Publishing, a leader in criminal justice publishing for more than 40 years. These imprints, along with the addition of Security Executive Council content, bring the work of highly regarded authors into one prestigious, complete collection.

The Security Executive Council (www.securityexecutivecouncil.com) is a leading problem-solving research and services organization focused on helping businesses builds value while improving their ability to effectively manage and mitigate risk. Drawing on the collective knowledge of a large community of successful security practitioners, experts, and strategic alliance partners, the Council develops strategy and insight and identifies proven practices that cannot be found anywhere else. Their research, services, and tools are focused on protecting people, brand, information, physical assets, and the bottom line.

Elsevier (www.elsevier.com/permissions) is an international multimedia publishing company that provides world-class information and innovative solutions tools. It is part of Reed Elsevier, a world-leading provider of professional information solutions in the science, medical, risk, legal, and business sectors.

Industry Applicability Validation

Industry applicability validation was performed by:

Randy Arnt, Executive Director of Global Security, Kimberly Clark

Edward G. Casey, Former Corporate Affiliation: Procter & Gamble; Security Executive Council Emeritus Faculty

Robert Dinsmore, Corporate Director, Systems and Security Controls, Baptist Health South Florida

John M. McCarthy, Former corporate affiliation: Texaco; Security Executive Council Emeritus Faculty

David Meunier, CISO, Cuna Mutual

Randy Uzzell, Former Corporate Affiliation: Burlington Industries; Security Executive Council Emeritus Faculty

Printed and bound by CPI Group (UK) Ltd, Croydon, CR0 4YY

08/05/2025

01864909-0001